EXPLORING WORLD CULTURES

France

Alicia Z. Klepeis

Cavendish Square
New York

Published in 2017 by Cavendish Square Publishing, LLC
243 5th Avenue, Suite 136, New York, NY 10016

Website: cavendishsq.com

This publication represents the opinions and views of the author based on his or her personal experience, knowledge, and research. The information in this book serves as a general guide only. The author and publisher have used their best efforts in preparing this book and disclaim liability rising directly or indirectly from the use and application of this book.

CPSIA Compliance Information: Batch #**CW17CSQ**

All websites were available and accurate when this book was sent to press.

Library of Congress Cataloging-in-Publication Data

Names: Klepeis, Alicia, 1971- author.
Title: France / Alicia Z. Klepeis.
Description: New York : Cavendish Square Publishing, [2017] | Series:
Exploring world cultures | Includes bibliographical references and index.
| Description based on print version record and CIP data provided by
publisher; resource not viewed.
Identifiers: LCCN 2016023841 (print) | LCCN 2016022255 (ebook) |
ISBN 9781502621450 (ebook) | ISBN 9781502621429 (paperback) |
ISBN 9781502621436 (6 pack) | ISBN 9781502621443 (Library bound)
Subjects: LCSH: France--Juvenile literature.
Classification: LCC DC17 (print) | LCC DC17 .K44 2017 (ebook) | DDC 944--dc23
LC record available at https://lccn.loc.gov/2016023841

Editorial Director: David McNamara
Editor: Kristen Susienka
Copy Editor: Rebecca Rohan
Associate Art Director: Amy Greenan
Designer: Joseph Macri
Production Coordinator: Karol Szymczuk
Photo Research: J8 Media

Printed in the United States of America

Contents

Introduction

France is a country in Western Europe. It has lots of special traditions and celebrations. People have lived in France for a very long time. During its history, many different people have ruled France. The country belonged to the Roman Empire for hundreds of years. Today, France's government is a **democracy**. It is a free country.

People in France work many different jobs. Some work in hospitals or hotels. Others make cars or airplanes in big factories. French people also create stylish clothes and grow food on farms.

France is a country with many beautiful places. It has beaches, forests, rivers, and islands. Visitors come from around the world to see France's amazing scenery. People also visit its cities, especially Paris.

The French enjoy music and the arts. Many famous artists have come from France. People in France also love good food. France is a wonderful country to explore.

Sailboats and yachts dot the turquoise waters of France's Azure coast.

France is a little smaller than the state of Texas and covers 210,026 square miles (543,965 square kilometers). It shares borders with eight other countries: Andorra, Belgium, Germany, Italy, Luxembourg, Monaco,

Black dots mark the country's many cities on this map of France.

Spain, and Switzerland. The Atlantic Ocean borders France to the west. The Mediterranean Sea borders France to the south.

France has a **diverse** landscape. The northern and western parts of the country have

FACT!

At 634 miles (1,020 km) long, the Loire is France's longest river.

wide plains. These areas are good for farming. The Alps and Pyrenees are tall mountain ranges in eastern and southern France.

Much of France has warm summers and cool winters. Southern France has mild winters and dry, sunny summers. France's mountainous areas are cooler. The peaks can be snow-covered all year round.

France's Plants and Animals

France has many kinds of plants and animals. Alpine marmots, red deer, and even flamingos live here. France's fields of lavender and wildflowers are beautiful.

People have lived in what is now France for a long time. Some of humans' earliest ancestors lived here about two million years ago. At first, they hunted and gathered their food.

Jean Victor Schnetz's painting shows a conflict from Parisian history.

Later, they settled down to farm and to raise animals.

Over two thousand years ago, the Romans occupied this area. They called it Gaul. Many different tribes attacked this territory. These groups of people included the Visigoths, the Vandals, and the Franks.

A Powerful Emperor

Napoleon Bonaparte was a French army general who crowned himself emperor of France in 1804. During his reign, France gained lots of new territories.

For about a thousand years, many powerful kings ruled France. But France's people grew tired of these kings. A violent period known as the French Revolution began in 1789. During this time, poor French citizens fought to get equal rights for all people.

In 1792, France became a **republic**. Today, the French vote for their leaders just like Americans do. France's leaders are the president and the prime minister.

FACT!

France got its name from the Franks, a group of people that invaded the area in the 400s CE.

Government

France is a democracy. The main part of France is in Europe, but the country also has smaller regions overseas. Mainland France is divided into thirteen regions. France's capital is Paris.

Paris's Luxembourg Palace

France's government has three parts:

1) legislative: This part of the government is known as Parliament. The members of Parliament write new laws.

2) judicial: The courts form this part of the government. They follow a document called a constitution. It describes all of France's basic laws.

French citizens can vote when they are eighteen years old. All eligible voters *must* vote in elections for members of the Senate.

3) executive: The president, prime minister, and a group called the Council of Ministers make up this part of the government.

The Parliament is made up of two parts. The Senate has 348 members. The National Assembly has 577 members. The Senate meets in the Luxembourg Palace to pass laws. This building is in Paris, the nation's capital.

FACT!

As of 2014, 26 percent of France's parliament members were women.

The Economy

France has the one of the world's biggest economies. The country trades with nations around the world. Like many countries in Europe, France's money is the euro.

Tourism is a big part of France's economy.

Working is important in France. Many people work in hotels and museums, and as tour guides. Other people have jobs in banks, hospitals, and shops. Almost one-quarter of French people work in factories. They make lots of different products, like aircrafts, electronics, cars, and food products. France is also famous for its excellent quality clothing and shoes.

Solar Power

In 2015, the largest solar park in Europe opened in Cestas, France. The plant provides enough power for three hundred thousand people.

French farmers grow many different crops, such as wine grapes and sugar beets. France also produces dairy products. Its cheese is celebrated around the world.

Tourism is an important part of France's economy. Every year, more people visit France than any other country in the world.

FACT!

France is known for its fashion. Chanel, Dior, and Givenchy are all famous French clothing designers.

The Environment

The plants, animals, and people of France need clean air and clean water to live. But not everywhere in France has these things. In cities like Paris, traffic creates pollution.

This photo shows air pollution around the Eiffel Tower and Paris rooftops.

FACT!

Organic farms are becoming more popular in France. These farms do not use bad chemicals to help their food grow.

Lots of different animals and plants live in France. Sadly, some French animals and plants are **endangered**. The Aran rock lizard is only found in a small area on the border of France and Spain.

France gets about 75 percent of its energy from **nuclear** sources. This is the most of any country in the world. One problem with nuclear energy involves removing its waste. Experts are working to find a way to get rid of this waste without hurting the environment.

The Cruas nuclear power plant

School Lunches in France

Kids in France eat meals at school. They aren't allowed to bring lunches from home. Less trash is created and less food is wasted in French schools.

The Ring of Kenza, a patisserie in Paris

Over sixty-two million people live in France. It is one of Europe's most populated countries.

Most French citizens are of French ancestry. However, France is a diverse country. It's hard to know a French person's heritage for certain. France has laws stopping others from collecting information about people's race or ethnic background. However, people of many different **ethnic groups** call France home.

With a population of over ten million people, Paris is France's largest city.

People have moved to France from all over the world. In the 1950s and 1960s, lots of people came to France from its overseas colonies such as Algeria and Morocco. In January 2014, about 8.9 percent of the people living in France were immigrants. Many of these groups have their own special traditions.

France's Aging Population

In 2015, almost 19 percent of France's people were sixty-five or older. This number is expected to rise to about 25 percent by 2030.

French people live in different ways. Almost 80 percent of people in France live in cities and towns. Their way of living is different from how people live in the countryside. French city-dwellers

The cityscape of Lyon is colorful and has beautiful buildings.

might live in an old house built centuries ago. Or they might live in a modern apartment building. Some people take the subway or drive cars to work. Others walk or bike to their jobs in schools, businesses, or factories. Families living in the city often have cell phones and computers.

The Mighty Metro

Paris's subway system, called the Metro, is the second busiest in Europe. Over six million people ride it each day.

Life in France's rural areas is often quiet and slow-paced. Small villages dot the landscape. People may grow crops and raise animals for food. Some farms offer visitors the chance to stay and experience country life in France.

A field of sunflowers in Verdon Natural Regional Park

French women used to stay home to look after their children and their house. Today, many women work as bankers, lawyers, teachers, or businesspeople.

FACT!

About 3.5 percent of French workers are employed in agriculture.

Religion

France has no official religion. All French people are free to believe in what they want. Still, religion is important to many French people. Over 60 percent of France's people are Christian. Most French citizens are Roman

A woman prays at a grave in a cemetery in Île-de-France, a region in north-central France.

Lourdes

Millions of people travel to Lourdes, France, each year. It is believed that in 1858 the Blessed Virgin Mary appeared here to a young French girl named Bernadette Soubirous. People come to Lourdes's spring to be healed.

More than fourteen million people visit Paris's Notre Dame cathedral each year.

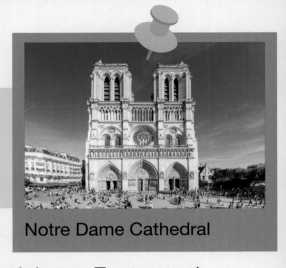

Notre Dame Cathedral

Catholic. Catholics in France celebrate Easter and Christmas. They also celebrate All Saints' Day (called Toussaint) on November 1. This holiday honors the dead. Many families visit their relatives' graves on that day.

In addition to Christians, about 7 to 9 percent of French people are Muslim. They worship in places called mosques. There are also small groups of Jews in France. More than 20 percent of France's people don't practice any religion.

Language

French is the official language of France. The country's government, businesses, and schools use this language. It is also the most commonly spoken language in France. About 88 percent of French people speak French as their first language.

This sign is written in French, English and Spanish.

Some people in France speak languages other than French. In northeastern France some folks speak Flemish. Along France's border with

Learn a Little French

If you want to ask someone you meet "How are you?" say, "Comment ça va?" (pronounced Kom-mon sa VA?)

Spain, some people speak a language called Basque. Arabic is also spoken in France. It is an especially popular language among immigrants from North Africa and the Middle East.

French people often learn to speak more than one language. Students usually learn English, Spanish, or German as their second language at school. The government is making an effort to have children start learning these languages at a younger age in the future.

FACT!

About 3 percent of people in France speak versions of the German language.

Arts and Festivals

France is a country that celebrates the arts. Many famous artists have come from France. Auguste Renoir and Paul Gauguin are well-known French painters.

A military parade on Bastille Day in July 2012

Music is another important art form in France. Many classical composers are French. Claude Debussy is a well-known example. He wrote a song called "Claire de Lune." Today, French musicians create new music, including jazz, rap, and rock.

Throughout France, there are festivals all year round. Some celebrate religious or historical

Carnival in Nice

Carnival is celebrated in the spring. The Carnival festival in Nice features decorated floats, people in colorful costumes, bands, and fireworks.

events. France also has several national holidays. People in France celebrate Bastille Day, known as *la fête national*, on July 14. This holiday marks the day that people stormed a prison called the Bastille. All over France, people celebrate with fireworks, military parades, and dancing.

FACT!

The average worker in France has thirty days of paid vacation each year.

Fun and Play

There are many ways to have fun in France. People in France enjoy sports. The country's most popular sport is soccer. But the French enjoy many other sports too. Tennis and

Les Menuires is a popular French ski resort.

bicycling are also well liked. People around the globe watch the Tour de France bicycle race held each July. During the winter, people ski at resorts in the Alps and the Pyrenees.

FACT!

France is home to Europe's most-visited theme park, Disneyland Paris.

26

Many people in France like to play games. A very popular game is lawn bowling, known as *boules* in French. The object of the game is to throw or roll a heavy ball as close as possible to a small target ball.

A group of women play the traditional game of *boules*.

Schoolchildren in France play lots of different games. Dodgeball, jump rope, tag, and hopscotch are popular on the playground. Some kids also enjoy playing jacks or marbles.

Beach-Lover's Paradise

France has many beautiful beaches. Seaside resorts on the Mediterranean include Cannes and Saint-Tropez.

Food

A French market stall offers many varieties of French cheese.

France is a country known for its food. People all over France love their food. It is common to shop at special stores for specific food items. For example, French shoppers might buy cheese at the *fromagerie* (cheese shop) and bread at the *boulangerie* (bakery). France also has big supermarkets. However, many folks prefer shopping daily at local shops or markets.

Over one thousand kinds of cheese are made in France.

French people eat lots of kinds of foods.
Fish is common to eat in areas near the sea.
A traditional French dish is escargot, or snails.
People often eat them with butter and garlic.
Bouillabaisse, or fish soup, is another popular dish.
The French also enjoy meals containing chicken,
beef, and rabbit. Ratatouille is a stew containing
zucchini, peppers, and eggplant.

People in France often drink coffee and tea.
Hot chocolate is popular at breakfast time. Some
folks also like fruit juice and soda.

Wine in France

France produces many kinds of wine.
Adults often enjoy a glass of wine with
their meals.

Glossary

democracy   A system of government in which leaders are chosen by the people.

diverse   Differing from one another.

endangered   Threatened with extinction.

ethnic group   Communities or populations made up of people who share a common cultural background or descent.

nuclear   Related to the energy that involves a nuclear fission or fusion reaction.

republic   A government that has a leader who is not a king or queen and is usually a president.

Find Out More

Books

Peppas, Lynn. *Cultural Traditions in France*. Cultural Traditions in My World. New York: Crabtree Publishing Company, 2014.

Savery, Annabel. *France*. Been There! Mankato, MN: Smart Apple Media, 2012.

Website

National Geographic: France

http://kids.nationalgeographic.com/explore/countries/france/#france-eiffel-tower.jpg

Video

BBC: A Primary School in Marseille

http://www.bbc.co.uk/education/clips/zcdg9j6

In this video, French children show what it's like to go to school in France.

Index

About the Author

Alicia Z. Klepeis began her career at the National Geographic Society. She is the author of many kids' books, including *The World's Strangest Foods*, *Bizarre Things We've Called Medicine*, *Francisco's Kites*, and *From Pizza to Pisa*. She lives with her family in upstate New York.